Contribitors

S. Atenzi
Ron Root
Gary Douglas
Akshat Lamba
J. Dawson Williams, D. Min.
Bjorn Leeson
Candy Wolff
Daniel Maunz
Emil Rem
Gary B. Haley
Jenna Greene
Takıya Smith
Alison Mcbain
Kelly Florence and Meg Hafdahl
Ryan Schuette
Allan Low
Ian P. Eviston
Michelle Bulriss
Patricia Skipper
Tshekedi Wallace
Thomas Richard Spradlin
Dr. Colleen Huber

Review Tales
A Book Magazine For Indie Authors

Founder & Editor in Chief: S. Jeyran Main
Publisher: Review Tales Publishing & Editing Services
Print & Distribution: Ingram Spark
Designs: Pexels
ISBN 978-1-988680-50-7 (Paperback)
ISBN 978-1-988680-51-4 (Digital)
www.jeyranmain.com
For all inquiries, please contact us directly.

TABLE OF CONTENTS

www.jeyranmain.com

Editor's Note

Dear Readers,

As the sun reaches its zenith and the days stretch longer, we're thrilled to bring you an exciting collection of articles that delve into the heart of the literary world. This edition is a treasure trove of insights, reflections, and candid conversations with writers, publishers, and industry experts.

Our contributing writers kick off this edition by sharing their experiences and valuable lessons learned as publishers. These narratives offer a rare glimpse into the intricate dance of balancing creativity and commerce, providing aspiring publishers with a roadmap of what to expect and how to thrive in the dynamic world of publishing.

For fans and writers of science fiction and fantasy, we explore the unique challenges these genres face. From world-building to genre conventions, our contributors discuss the hurdles and triumphs of writing in realms that defy the ordinary and push the boundaries of imagination.

One of the most compelling pieces in this edition tackles the pervasive issue of systemic prejudice and discrimination in the writing industry. Through powerful testimonies and thoughtful analysis, we highlight the ongoing struggles and the efforts to create a more inclusive and equitable literary community.

Our author interviews are, as always, a highlight. This season, we sit down with some of the most innovative voices in literature. These conversations provide a window into their creative processes, inspirations, and the journeys that shape their stories.

The influence of AI on creativity and the writing community is another pivotal topic we explore. As technology continues to evolve, its impact on the literary world is profound. Our articles examine both the opportunities and challenges AI presents, and how authors are navigating this new landscape.

We also delve into the balancing act between genre and academic writing. This discussion is crucial for writers striving to maintain authenticity and scholarly integrity while crafting compelling narratives that captivate readers.

Finally, we touch on the concept of "Author Therapy" during book promotion. This unique perspective offers strategies for managing the often overwhelming process of bringing a book to market, ensuring that authors can maintain their well-being and enthusiasm throughout the promotional journey.

As you dive into this edition, we hope you find inspiration, enlightenment, and a sense of camaraderie with fellow readers and writers. Here's to a summer filled with stories that challenge, entertain, and transform.

Happy reading!

Sincerely,

Jeyran Main

Editor-in-Chief
Review Tales Magazine

Almost Ten Years of Reading Furiously: What I Learned as a Publisher

by S. Atzeni

Next year, our publishing house, Read Furiously, will turn ten years old. That's almost a decade of publishing authors we admire and books we care about. It's also almost a decade of sleepless nights, no weekends, panic attacks, and constant planning. And it's almost a decade of having the enormous privilege of carrying our authors' dreams alongside our own.

We created Read Furiously out of a need for change, to create a space where writers of all experiences can exist without worrying about the mainstream sensibilities that govern larger publishing companies. Over these nearly ten years, I've learned much about myself as an author, editor, and publisher. I learned that the skillset, opportunity, and idea will show up when they're good and ready. I also learned that the publishing industry is still very uneven. The best intentions cannot protect you from gatekeepers, even at an indie level. I've been ghosted, ignored, laughed at, and (my personal favorite) rejected before I could get in the door. However, I've also been welcomed by beautiful members of the literary community: bookstores, mentors, coaches, other presses, and authors. Can't find the community or space that you need to thrive as a creative? Build your own. It's messy, but the beautiful journey makes up indie publishing. We all have so much good work and trouble to get into.

When we published our first title, the graphic novel series The MOTHER Principle, almost ten years ago, we had no idea that Read Furiously would expand to a roster of talented and award-winning authors, two bestselling series, and over fifty books by 2026. Nor did we anticipate that we would continue to publish books during a global pandemic. Or that we would lose one of our beloved authors and biggest supporters, Christopher Bursk, in 2021. Or that people would recognize our books and our publisher logo. Like all great stories, we have no idea what will happen next, but it's exciting to wake up every day and turn to the next page.

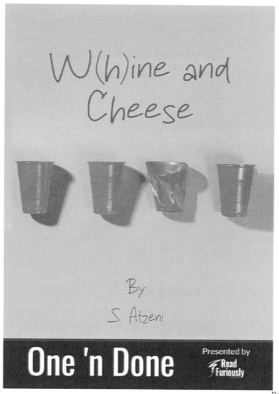

Sci-fi Fantasy Challenges

by Ron Root

Writing novels has been a lifelong goal that I've finally taken the time to pursue. Years ago, while flying from Oregon to Florida, I realized I had no book to read. Stopping at an airport bookstore, I bought a Terry Brooks fantasy novel and got lost in its story. So much so that a story of my own popped into my mind. That story haunted me so much that I put it into short story form. Then, over the years, it grew into a fully-fledged novel that became *Nexus Moons*, the first in my *Tales of Graal* series. Having read J.R.R. Tolkien's *Lord of the Rings* trilogy, I decided I needed to write at least two more. *Kin's Quest* is the follow-on novel that continues the saga of *Nexus Moons'* hero. The third book in the series will continue the saga of characters introduced in the first two books.

Writing sci-fi fantasies presents challenges not faced in other genres. Given that the story world is fantastical and unfamiliar to your readers, the author must meticulously build it so it can be envisioned. *The Tales of Graal* is set in the equivalent of our own Middle Ages and, therefore, must accurately portray that period. The trickiest aspect is language. Any modern word can jolt the reader out of the story, which forces the author to meticulously evaluate each word's etymology. My litmus test is that words must have been in use prior to 1600. Like other genres, character arc, overall story, and chapter structure must still be carefully honed. Although it's work, it's a labor of love. Once done, few things are more satisfying than learning someone has read and enjoyed your creation. If you read this series, hopefully, the same can be said of you.

Ron retired after 50 years in IT. He started writing in his thirties, developing a two-book series with a third in progress. He enjoys tournament bridge and whitewater rafting. Ron is a father of five, grandfather of seven, and lives with his wife in the Pacific Northwest.

Allowance: A Key to Total Freedom

by Gary Douglas

Allowance is a concept not often discussed, yet it is crucial for achieving total freedom and creating everything you desire in life. Simply put, allowance means refraining from judging things as right or wrong, good or bad. Each point of view you encounter is just an interesting perspective.

Practicing allowance is beneficial in many ways. It provides a pragmatic approach to understanding the dynamics of your family and opens the door to possibilities you may never have considered. Allowance grants you the freedom to choose and create beyond the limitations that others believe to be true in all areas of your life.

When you choose to be in allowance, you begin to liberate yourself from the judgments that have been restricting you, whether these judgments are your own or those of others. Being in allowance means keeping your eyes open and your awareness engaged to assist you as you navigate your life's path.

Here's how you can start shifting your points of view and increase your allowance for everything in your life:

Observe Your Perspectives: Pay attention to your existing viewpoints and start seeing them as merely "interesting" rather than absolute truths. For example, if you are frustrated with your finances and believe that wealthy people are unhappy, this belief will limit your financial potential. Simply repeat to yourself, "Interesting point of view. I have that point of view." Continue saying this until the energy of the viewpoint shifts. You'll know

it has shifted when you start feeling lighter. This sense of lightness indicates that your perspective has changed, and your experience can change too. This transformation exemplifies allowance in action—a simple concept with life-altering results.

Gary Douglas, author of "The Gift of Allowance," founded Access Consciousness, a global personal development company. He also launched the eco-retreat El-Lugar in Costa Rica and owns ventures in Australia, Italy, and Texas. Gary promotes greater consciousness and possibilities. www.garymdouglas.com

WHY AND WHEN I BEGAN?

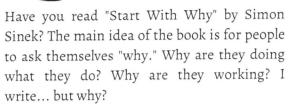

by Akshat Lamba

Have you read "Start With Why" by Simon Sinek? The main idea of the book is for people to ask themselves "why." Why are they doing what they do? Why are they working? I write... but why?

I'm so lucky that my best friend in sixth grade wanted to write a story. It was such a random moment. Because of him, I thought of writing one too. He wrote a comic; I wrote a short story. I laugh when I recall that because what I did was so foolish. I tore a few middle pages from my notebook, crafted a cover, wrote a synopsis, and used each page as a chapter. I wrote a story called 'Take Care.' It was cringy, but I realized—I enjoyed writing so much! And that's how it started. I began writing what I thought was trash. And I wrote a lot of it. I even wrote a novel just for practice. There were times when I stopped writing for various reasons, but I always picked it up again, sometimes after years. It wasn't until COVID-19 that I fully engaged myself in it and discovered that this was something I truly loved to do.

The thing was, I loved "Harry Potter," and I used to wonder, how can someone create such a beautiful story? It was all imagination, with such detail. It was so heart-touching. And I wanted to create something like that. I still do. I aim to write such beautiful stories.

My short story "Cotton In A Sea Of Blood" is now available for pre-order on Amazon. I wish to share it as widely as I can. I hope to give readers the same feeling of awe and wonder and to touch their hearts. And this is why I write.

I'm Akshat Lamba, a Delhi-based writer. Harry Potter fascinated and inspired me as a child, sparking a desire to create awe-inspiring tales. As an adult, Game of Thrones further fueled my passion for storytelling. My goal is to craft meaningful narratives that provoke wonder, touch hearts, and feature authentic characters. That's the gift I want to share with the world.

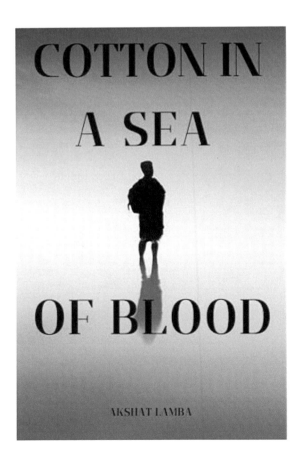

My Words and How I Deal with the Writing Industry

by J. Dawson Williams, D. Min.

Have you ever felt mysteriously drawn to a particular assignment? If so, did you follow your passion? Did you respond because you felt a sense of vocation or a calling to that assignment? My book, *Overcoming Systemic Prejudice and Discrimination: Achieving Success Through Ethical Resilience*, emerged from an unshakeable desire to help overcome prejudicial behavior and its devastating effects.

My typical writing style involves selecting a subject, gathering resources, organizing the material, dedicating some time to writing, and then quickly completing the project. In contrast, this writing project took decades. Year after year, my efforts to force this book to completion resulted in failure.

Information and ideas for my book flooded in from observations I made in counseling, coaching, and consulting work. My clarity gradually evolved as random insights surfaced. My only option was to take copious notes and file them away. Eventually, those files began to take shape with titles that became chapter headings.

Finally, one early spring morning, I woke up well before daylight, sensed that it was time, and began to write. This drive to write continued for weeks. My concepts, notes, files, and other resource materials started coming together as cohesive content. A manuscript was in the hands of an editor within weeks, and the publication process was underway!

I view any "less than positive" reviewer comments as constructive criticism. Interestingly, it's worth noting that other reviewers offer incredibly positive feedback regarding the very features negatively cited by others. I am thankful that most reviewers critique my book as relevant, potent, beneficial, and eye-opening.

I self-published the book and am aware of the need to produce a companion work that further develops my subtitle, "Achieving Success Through Ethical Resilience." So, it may be that my passion is indeed my vocation.

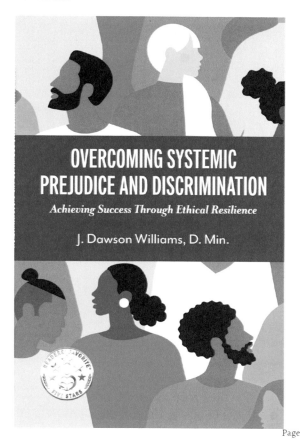

Author Interview

BJORN LEESSON

When did you first realize you wanted to be a writer?

Originally, I don't think I consciously pursued being a writer. I have always been fascinated with dozens and dozens of topics, and putting my thoughts about these topics in written form was always a natural impulse for me. Writing seems to be the most efficient and purest form of communicating those thoughts for me, much more so than verbal communication. Eventually, my interests shifted from non-fiction and technical works to fiction, and that is when it dawned on me, "Hey, I could possibly be a writer!"

How do you schedule your life when you're writing?

With great difficulty, to be honest. I have a more than full-time real-world job to feed myself, a hobby farm that my wife and I manage for our entertainment, and now I have an addiction to writing my stories. Time, as it turns out, is indeed limited, as my elders have always said—and I didn't believe them until now. But, as long as I feel it has a purpose, my writing is a part of my life, and it squeezes in where it can.

What would you say is your interesting writing quirk?

I absolutely insist that each character is "real" and distinctive, just like real people are in real life. I carefully develop each one with their own speaking styles, their own habits and quirks, and their own relationships to each other—sometimes good and sometimes bad. I spend much time trying to make my stories relatable and realistic.

Where did you get your information or idea for your book?

My own book series is a collective and melding of a hundred personal interests, my personal experiences with people, a sprinkle of every book I have ever read, a pinch of every movie I have ever watched, and my deepest thoughts of what the world is and what I wish it would be.

CANDY WOLFF

When did you first realize you wanted to be a writer?

When I came back from losing my husband in Cabo, it was very devastating. I had to tell my story over and over, and each time I did, I was told, "You really need to write a book." So, after three months of hearing so many people tell me I needed to write the book because my story could help others, I felt God was speaking to me. I took a big step and decided to do it.

How do you schedule your life when you're writing?

It was very difficult as I have a full-time job, and my youngest son is a senior in high school. He plays volleyball for both club and school teams, so between everything, I just had to schedule time to sit down and work on it.

How did you get your book published?

After completing the manuscript, I reached out to a few different publishing companies. I had the opportunity to talk with all of them and finally picked Kirk House Publishers because our values lined up. It has been such a pleasure working with them.

Where did you get your information or idea for your book?

My book is my life story of losing my husband unexpectedly while we were on vacation in Mexico for my 50th birthday. It is raw, real, and completely honest. It was difficult, but a great way to start my healing process.

Is there anything you would like to confess about as an author?

I must say, it's scary that I have opened my heart to tell my story. I just hope that my book resonates with the readers. It's hard that you put your whole heart, time, and money into it, and now I can only wait and see how things turn out.

DANIEL MAUNZ

When did you first realize you wanted to be a writer?

I've always enjoyed writing. In high school, a friend and I would routinely write scripts in science class, secretly passing it back and forth to take turns adding scenes. And when I first started dating my wife, I would regularly write her short stories to gift her on her birthday or Christmas (I was also on a limited budget back then …). It was only until I started my current job about ten years ago that I had the time and energy to devote to actually working on novels.

How do you schedule your life when you're writing?

I spend a lot of time thinking about what I want to write before sitting down to a keyboard. By doing so much "writing" in my head throughout the day, I'm in a great position to get a lot done when I can find twenty or thirty minutes to sit down and transcribe my thoughts. But even finding those small windows of time isn't always easy with a full-time job and a young child running around the home.

What would you say is your interesting writing quirk?

The plot of the story comes much later to me than it probably does to other writers. The first issue I tackle is deciding what overarching question I want my story to address. For example, my first book ("Questions of Perspective") addresses the meaning of life, whereas my follow-up book ("Hyphenated Relations") addresses the meaning of family. From there, I think about what characters and conflicts would be best for tackling those questions. Once that is determined, it is pretty straightforward to find a plot that suits my purposes.

How did you get your book published?

My first novel was not easy to pigeonhole into a specific genre, which made it difficult to find a publisher. That book is best described as metaphysical fiction, in that it explores a bitter attorney's quest to find the real purpose of life after he has a brush with God. But then I came across an independent publisher named Black Rose Writing, which takes great pride in publishing books of any genre, and it was a great fit for my book (and its follow-up).

EMIL REM

When did you first realize you wanted to be a writer?

In mid-primary school, at the age of nine. As an African immigrant fostered by an English family at the age of five, books were my escape and sanctuary. Once I could speak and read English, I devoured four large dictionaries, ticking off each word, learning its meaning and etymology. My love for the lyrical magic of words drove me to read every book in sight. "If those authors can do it, so can I."

What is your interesting writing quirk?

All the friends I sent each chapter to panned my writing style, calling it hopeless. My father, an airline employee, showered me with free tickets around the world. The trouble was, we had no money—no camera, minimal cash, no guidebooks. So, I had to live like the local poor. My mind was my video camera. This led to my stories being written in the third person rather than in the first. Although set in exotic locales, the stories hinged on the forgotten of the world that nobody noticed—the elderly yam seller at Dar-es-Salaam harbor or the nondescript Filipina nanny who sat beside me on a bus journey to Lefkosia in Cyprus. Nowhere in my writing was my name mentioned, nor was I ever described.

How did you get your stories published?

By blood, toil, sweat, and tears, with an unquenchable belief in my own destiny. My writing began at the age of 60. The first chapter of Chasing Aphrodite was the first piece of writing I ever created. I started with writing short stories as I had no idea when my inspiration would dry up and I would succumb to failure, my words turning to dust. One story led to another. After the sixth, my errant editor pronounced, "These are good enough to be published." And, one by one, they were in literary magazines across the world. Thus started my epic voyage.

GARY B. HALEY

How do you schedule your life when you're writing?

Are you kidding? There's no writing schedule. I am a stay-at-home dad for our three-year-old. I write spontaneously when I find a few moments.

Where did you get your information or idea for your book?

The concept for my Attunist Trilogy came from my defense industry experiences in Central America, Europe, and the Middle East. Writing about it all was cheaper than therapy.

What do you like to do when you're not writing?

My wife and I enjoy vacationing in places we've never been before. I've been to all 50 states and 16 countries. On the list: The Stonehenge sites, the Galapagos Islands, Iceland, and New Zealand.

What was one of the most surprising things you learned in creating your book?

Fortunately, I realized I'm not as angry as I was in the mid-to-late 1990s. A lot of what I wrote then was out of anger from all the horrific fallout caused by trying to combat terrorism and reduce drug trafficking into the United States. I began writing my Attunist Trilogy in 1998 after being out of the defense industry for three years. It took many years to muddle through all the memories and anger and create something entertaining yet revealing.

(The writing therapy was obviously successful. I've resolved most of the anger and allowed it to fade.)

How do you process and deal with negative book reviews?

About 10% of the population is habitually negative—one out of every 10. So, if less than 10% of my reviews are negative, I consider myself on the curve's positive side. Also, if you have anything worthwhile to say, someone or some group will invariably disagree with you or object to your insights. The takeaway is, don't worry about the negativity. Besides, two or three negative reviews often work in an author's favor, as people read the negative reviews and wholeheartedly disagree.

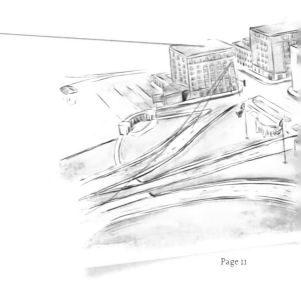

JENNA GREENE

When did you first realize you wanted to be a writer?

I knew I wanted to be a writer at such an early age that I can't even put a time or date to it. The idea has always been there, that I was destined to be an author. Whether I wanted to be a fairy princess, teacher, zoologist, or anything else, the phrase "and a writer" was always attached as well.

How do you schedule your life when you're writing?

I'm not like other authors – though, really, who is? I have a very busy job, with work, parenting, coaching, and volunteer responsibilities. There's almost no possibility that I can find 3-4 hours to write in one sitting. But I manage an hour a few nights a week. Any words on the page are progress, and I don't judge myself if I get a lot of writing done one month and not much the rest. Because I am a teacher, I can find more freedom to write in the summer, which helps.

Where did you get your information or idea for your book?

Each book has its own journey, with a different motive for creation, or inspiration. I've written books based on a dream, a real incident, a 'what if' that popped into a conversation, a meme – you name it! Creative people are always thinking, dreaming, and wondering. I think everyone does, actually, but writers take it a step further and record their thoughts as tales.

What do you like to do when you're not writing?

I dance during the year, with my preferred styles being jive and Broadway. During the spring and summer months, I dedicate my time to dragon boat coaching, paddling, and drumming. I love being on the water! There's not much time for other pursuits, though I do get to write and direct school plays and concerts through my work as a teacher.

TAKIYAH SMITH

When did you first realize you wanted to be a writer?

I came up with the name, "Single Mom and the City." Approximately six months later, I decided I wanted to write a book on the topic of motherhood. This was around 2017.

How do you schedule your life when you're writing?

I like to maintain flexibility in my schedule. My main goal when writing is to write daily for at least 15 minutes. While I typically write for thirty minutes to an hour, I like to set a manageable goal to ensure that I write daily.

How did you get your book published?

After interviewing several publishers and getting feedback from authors published by large publishing houses, I decided to self-publish. One caveat I often observed with self-published works was that they "looked" self-published. I was determined to publish a book that looked professionally done. I spent countless hours transforming my book from manuscript to published work. I was very pleased with the results, and others were too. A friend who had written a book was so blown away by what I had created that he hired me as a consultant so that he too could self-publish his manuscript. Out of that, a business was born.

Where did you get your information or idea for your book?

The information stemmed from my own experiences as well as from experts and statistical data.

How do you process and deal with negative book reviews?

I value constructive feedback. But if I'm honest, I haven't really had any negative feedback outside of comments like, "the book is for everyone, not just single moms," which I agree with. I put so much time, attention, and research into my book that one would be hard-pressed to criticize its content. Much of what's in my book is backed by statistics, and numbers don't lie.

AUTHOR VERSUS AI

ALISON MCBAIN

AI is on every writer's mind. Some authors use it; some eschew it. It can spark a very heated debate in literary circles. Try it for yourself—go up to a group of writers and ask them: "AI... good or bad?" You'll probably have everyone lined up around the block, ready to share their opinion.

I'm not here to debate the merits of AI. In fact, I'm here to show that it's something that doesn't even need to be debated. Instead, it can be conquered like the evil villain from a comic book. That's what I'm doing in my current project, Author Versus AI, where I'm writing a book each week for a year.

The goal? To show that authors can write nearly as fast (but much better) than any old computer program.

Here's how I'm able to write a book in a week and how you can too:

1) Preparation. Before I begin a manuscript, I've already completed a synopsis, chapter-by-chapter outline, and character sketches.

2) Habit. Sitting down for several solid hours each day and doing it at the same time each day helps my writer's brain realize: "Hey, it's 9 a.m. Time to put words on the page!"

3) Daily goal. Every day, I have a goal I'd like to reach. It might be 5,000 words or 3 chapters or similar. I sit down and don't stop until I meet that goal (except for tea and sometimes chocolate).

4) Permission to fail. This last item sounds like a contradiction, but I don't beat myself up if I don't complete my goal for that day. By not guilting myself over not finishing, it helps me avoid the instinct to procrastinate, which is the death knell for any project. Positive thinking is key: tomorrow is a new day. So, if you'd like to show AI who the boss is, join me and tackle this challenge of writing a book in a week. Follow these steps and get to writing. Good luck!

ACADEMIC VS GENRE WRITING: FINDING YOUR BALANCE

KELLY FLORENCE AND MEG HAFDAHL

When we met over twenty years ago, it was our love of the horror genre that bonded us. We spent weekends watching zombie movies, writing stage plays about aliens, and daydreaming about making our mark in horror. Alternatively, we were both drawn to academia. Kelly pursued higher education in theater and communications and became a tenured professor at Lake Superior College in Duluth, MN. Meg studied literature and is currently a creative writing student at Oxford University in the UK. We have written a non-fiction series, *The Science of Horror*, which explores the tenuous intersections of pop science, true crime, film history, cheeky humor, and our own biographies. Drawing from varied experiences has been fulfilling but also challenging.

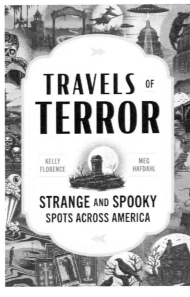

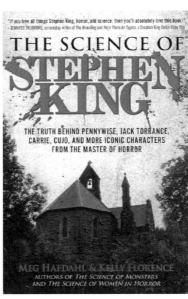

As mentioned, Kelly's theater background has aided us in our screenwriting (we've received several award nominations for horror TV pilot scripts). Meg, a fiction writer with published novels and short stories, has used her experience to develop story structures in our real encounters for our upcoming travel book, *Travels of Terror: Strange and Spooky Spots Across America* (coming September 2024). Even Meg's academic instruction in poetry at Oxford can illuminate words or theory to make her a better writer in any prose situation. When Kelly instructs her students through essays, she, too, is learning from teaching.

Plus, we learn as we work with agents, editors, and publishers. One challenge we've encountered is balancing genre and academic writing in our fictional work. This is a personal preference that a writer must tweak to their liking. If you are writing in a genre, whether it's a spy thriller or a Victorian romance, there are tropes your readers expect. And if you write it, we assume you must enjoy these tropes, too! Yet, in academia, there are often more subtleties, perhaps less "obvious" story endings, even deaths or uncomfortable happenings that genre fiction wouldn't consider "sellable." These are ineffable things that are often not considered when writing, and we encourage you to consider them!

AN END TO KINGS

BY RYAN SCHUETTE

Writing a novel is a relentless challenge. To achieve traditional publication, you'll need more than talent and a good story. You'll need people skills, knowledge of current trends, persistence, and self-belief.

I understand the importance of these elements. This month, I'm publishing An End to Kings, the sequel to A Seat for the Rabble and the second book in my award-winning series A King Without a Crown. It's been over nine years since I dedicated myself to this childhood dream, starting in my grad-school dorm, inspired by epic stories like those of George R.R. Martin.

For aspiring traditional authors, here's what I've learned over nearly a decade:

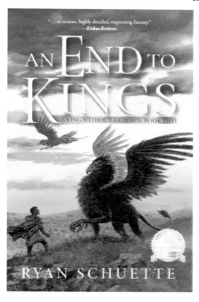

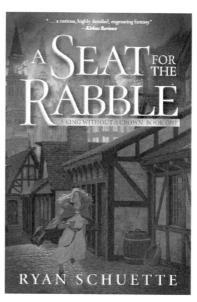

1- Invest in Publishing Knowledge: Publishing is a hypercompetitive business. Literary agents receive countless queries, so understanding the "chain of persuasion" is crucial. Your work must sell. Consider courses from Writer's Digest University to learn from agents directly.

2- Know Your Genre: Read extensively within your genre, focusing on recent publications. Agents' tastes follow industry trends, and readers' preferences change frequently. Reading widely will enhance your writing, inspire you, and keep you informed. Use recent comparisons in your query letter to strengthen your case.

3- Master the Query Letter: A compelling query letter is essential for finding a literary agent. It must pitch your story succinctly and include relevant comparisons.

By staying informed about publishing trends and your genre, you'll save time and frustration, improve your novel, and connect with agents more effectively. Persist and refine your people skills.

"DUMB" ORPHANS: THE BUNDU BUNCH TRILOGY
Allan Low

Reviewer: Jeyran Main

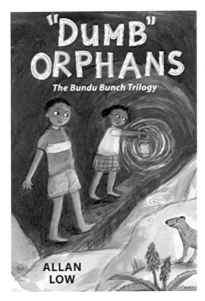

Allan Low's "Dumb" Orphans: The Bundu Bunch Trilogy enters the young adult literary scene with a title that immediately provokes controversy. The word "dumb," although enclosed in quotation marks, sets a confrontational tone that might unsettle some readers, as it did me. The book claims these orphans are labeled as such by their community due to their inability to afford schooling, while paradoxically showcasing their ingenuity, which starkly contrasts with the title's implication.

Despite the off-putting title, the book is engaging and holds substantial educational value, making it an excellent choice for nightly reading sessions and classroom discussions. It could particularly serve as a starting point for dialogues about language use and societal perceptions.

The trilogy is neatly packaged into one volume, comprising three books. Book I, "Aiyasha's Bottomless Briefcase," introduces a group of young orphans guided by the slightly older Aiyasha, reminiscent of the dynamics in the Boxcar Children series. The narrative, through Sipho's eyes, effectively uses their day-to-day challenges to illustrate how necessity sparks creativity.

Book II, "Aiyasha's Appeal," switches narrators to Elah, an orphan who travels to England with Aiyasha. This installment transitions into a setting akin to a non-magical Hogwarts, providing a fresh backdrop while continuing the theme of overcoming adversity.

The final segment, Book III, "Aiyasha's Magical Legacy," follows the orphans into adulthood, focusing on their college years and beyond, aiming to fulfill Aiyasha's vision for their homeland. This narrative arc resembles the mature reflections in Cry the Beloved Country, yet the reading level feels somewhat mismatched with the earlier sections, potentially challenging younger readers.

A critical flaw in the series is the inconsistent timeline and character development, which may confuse readers about the characters' ages and progression. However, the series excels in its depiction of Southern African culture, moral lessons, and the pivotal role of family, complemented by flawless grammar and enriching illustrations.

In conclusion, despite the initial missteps with the title, "Dumb" Orphans offers a rich, culturally informative experience that merits a five-star rating for its depth and educational potential. This trilogy is a commendable addition to young adult literature, capable of sparking important conversations and broadening worldviews.

DEMONSLAYER
Ian P. Eviston

Reviewer: Jeyran Main

Ian P. Eviston's 'Demonslayer' captivates with its tale of Spirit Clayborn, a burgeoning warrior in the formidable Vanguard tasked with defending humanity against demonic forces. Set in a world where humans and demons have coexisted under a fragile peace treaty, the story erupts when the archdemon Xaxus threatens to unravel this uneasy truce. This plot sets the stage for an epic narrative rich in conflict and moral complexity.

The lore of the world is intricately designed around the concept of aether, a mystical substance integral to both humans and demons. The treaty's restriction on demons harvesting aether from humans leads to dire consequences within the demon community, including famine and riots. This adds layers of sympathy toward what are traditionally seen as antagonistic figures. This gray moral area is further explored through characters like Astaroth, an archdemon caught between loyalty and rebellion, enriching the narrative with internal conflict and philosophical debates about war, peace, and survival.

Spirit and his diverse group of allies, including Dimitri Valentine, Amelia Eldrid, Skylar, and Taya, are each well-crafted with distinct backgrounds and motivations. This diversity not only enriches their interactions but also mirrors the complexity of their world. Each character is drawn into the conflict with varying degrees of reluctance and bravado, making their journey not just one of external combat but also of internal growth.

Eviston's storytelling prowess shines throughout the book. The narrative is tightly woven with suspenseful twists and intense character showdowns that keep the pages turning. Moreover, the emotional depth—spanning love, loss, bravery, and betrayal—imbues the high-stakes adventure with heartfelt stakes.

'Demonslayer' is an excellent addition to the fantasy genre, offering a fresh take on the dynamics between humans and demons, coupled with a rich exploration of themes such as loyalty and the costs of war. I rate this book a perfect four out of four stars and eagerly anticipate the next installment in the series. It is a must-read for fans of fantasy looking for a new world to get lost in, where every character's choice can tip the balance of an age-old conflict.

SOCK LOBSTERS
Michelle Bulriss

Reviewer: Jeyran Main

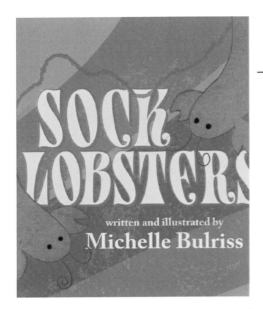

Michelle Bulriss's 'Sock Lobsters' is not just a children's book; it's a heartfelt journey through dealing with grief, wrapped in the warmth of a whimsical seaside adventure. The cover, bursting with beachy hues and adorned with charming, albeit impractical, animated socks, sets the tone for a story that is both magical and meaningful.

Bulriss, serving as both author and illustrator, brings a unique authenticity and cohesion to the story. Her background as an advocate for mental health and emotional intelligence infuses the narrative with a deep understanding of its themes. The illustrations boast graphic novel-esque clarity, with standout images like the realistically depicted post office and the Lobster Shack, cleverly reminiscent of a Red Lobster restaurant. The use of color is particularly striking—Sebastian the sock appears against a stark black background, symbolizing pessimism, while Lola radiates optimism against a backdrop of rainbows.

The structure of the book cleverly integrates the five stages of grief, with each stage denoted by the dark backgrounds on the pages, guiding both young readers and adults through a difficult subject with ease and understanding. This approach not only educates but also provides a framework to help adults discuss grief with children, aligning with the emotional journey of the sock characters, Sebastian and Lola.

One minor hiccup in this seamless narrative is a perplexing illustration on page 23—a side view of Bubbles the heroic cat on a grassy background—which momentarily disrupts the flow of the story, leaving readers puzzled about its inclusion.

Overall, 'Sock Lobsters' is superbly edited with no noticeable errors, and Bulriss's narrative technique—using socks as characters to explore heavy themes—is both innovative and endearing. This book is highly recommended for parents, educators, and counselors looking to introduce young children to the concepts of loss and recovery. The clever integration of a practical element, like the Sebastian lobster socks, adds an extra layer of engagement, embodying the book's ethos of empathy 'close to the sole.'

Sock Lobsters is a wonderfully crafted tale that respects its young audience's intelligence and emotional depth. It is both helpful and entertaining, and it succeeds in making the discussion of grief accessible and engaging for children.

DECEPTIVE
CALM

PATRICIA SKIPPER

DECEPTIVE CALM
Patricia Skipper

Reviewer: Jeyran Main

Patricia Skipper's Deceptive Calm delves into the complexities of racial identity and societal acceptance. Set against the backdrop of 1968, a pivotal year in American history marked by civil rights struggles and social upheaval, this novel compellingly explores the human desire for acceptance and the often painful journey toward self-identity.

The story opens with a dramatic and heart-wrenching incident: Trisha, a white girl, becomes the accidental victim of a Ku Klux Klan attack intended for her friend Vanessa, a Black woman whose light skin often leads others to mistake her for white. This tragic event sets the stage for a narrative rich in tension and emotional depth as Trisha's parents face the agonizing decision of whether to allow Dr. William Hale, a Black doctor, to perform life-saving surgery on their daughter.

Through the character of Vanessa, Skipper skillfully portrays the inner turmoil and identity struggles faced by individuals caught between different worlds. Vanessa's journey is self-discovery and resilience as she navigates societal prejudices while forging her own path and affirming her identity as a Black woman.

Trisha's character shines brightly in this narrative. Her unyielding loyalty and bravery, particularly in her efforts to protect Vanessa and her child, highlight the power of friendship and the lengths one will go to uphold it. These themes are further enriched by the character of Sis Rosalie, whose vibrant humor and quirky personality add layers of warmth and light-heartedness to the otherwise intense plot.

What stands out most in *Deceptive Calm* is its seamless integration of historical context with the personal stories of its characters, creating a narrative that is both educational and profoundly moving. The book is meticulously edited, with no distracting errors, allowing readers to fully immerse themselves in the beautifully crafted world Skipper has created.

This novel is a must-read for anyone interested in historical fiction, particularly those drawn to stories of racial identity, friendship, and the enduring human quest for belonging. Patricia Skipper's insightful storytelling and rich character development earn *Deceptive Calm* a well-deserved five out of five stars. It's a poignant reminder of the challenges and triumphs of the human spirit, making it a valuable addition to the shelves of all who cherish deep, thought-provoking literature.

THE TITAN CROWN
BY TSHEKEDI WALLACE

King Grandres of the Kalicos nation seeks the Titan Crown to establish his ultimate rule. However, Hetkarej, an evil Yatavra-System Lord, holds the crown. Grandres' nemesis, Queen Fasjey of the Reduzen race, shares the planet Daheza with him under the System Lords' mandate. The Kalicos and Reduzen races battle off-world for resources, while Supreme Lord Master Mocowas seeks to control both sides.

Fasjey, allied with the Lutresas and Giyehe, fights against Grandres' forces. Supported by his son Valeskin, Grandres plans to overthrow their enemies, including the System Lords.

The System Lords demand annual harvests and taxes to support their army. Pirates, led by Captain Ikizuni, aim to end the System Lords' reign, preparing for a historic war.

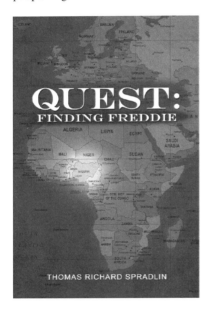

QUEST: FINDING FREDDIE:
BY THOMAS RICHARD SPRADLIN

"Quest: Finding Freddie" narrates a 1976 case handled by Richard Spradlin, a partner at the Washington, D.C. law firm Clifford & Warnke. The case involves searching for a client known as "Freddie," who vanished in Lagos, Nigeria, on August 14, 1976, during the Jewish Sabbath. Freddie's disappearance occurred shortly after the high-profile Entebbe rescue by Israeli forces, which had embarrassed Uganda's President Idi Amin.

At the time, Nigeria was also unstable due to a failed military coup on February 13, 1976, resulting in the assassination of General Murtala Muhammed. Amid this turmoil, Spradlin was dispatched by his firm to find Freddie.

NEITHER SAFE NOR EFFECTIVE
BY DR. COLLEEN HUBER

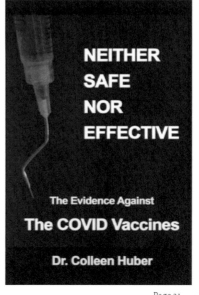

Governments in Europe and North America have released data on COVID-19 vaccine effects. Screenshots of these pages back up the material in this book. Are the COVID-19 vaccines safe?

Do they meet the Bradford Hill causation criteria for reported health events? What happened in the Pfizer and animal studies?

Colleen Huber, NMD, is a naturopathic medical doctor and expert witness in court cases involving vaccine safety. She compiles vital statistics and data from governments and vaccine manufacturers to prepare testimony.

Ensure you have all relevant information on COVID-19 vaccines before making your final decision.

Printed in the USA
CPSIA information can be obtained
at www.ICGtesting.com
CBRC090934070724
11197CB00024B/77